AT THE MERCY SEAT

AT THE
mercy
seat

Susan McCaslin

RONSDALE PRESS

AT THE MERCY SEAT
Copyright © 2003 Susan McCaslin

RONSDALE PRESS
3350 West 21st Avenue
Vancouver, B.C., Canada
V6S 1G7

Edited by Ronald B. Hatch
Typesetting: Julie Cochrane, in New Baskerville 11 pt on 13.5
Cover Art: Tracey Tarling, "Memory and Distance in Stillness Awash,"
    48" x 48", oil/mix/media on panel, 2002
Cover Design: Julie Cochrane
Author Photo: Mark Haddock
Paper: Ancient Forest Friendly Rolland "Enviro" — 100% post-consumer
    waste, totally chlorine-free and acid-free

Ronsdale Press wishes to thank the Canada Council for the Arts, the Government of Canada through the Book Publishing Industry Development Program (BPIDP), and the Province of British Columbia through the British Columbia Arts Council for their support of its publishing program.

National Library of Canada Cataloguing in Publication Data

McCaslin, Susan, 1947–
    At the mercy seat / Susan McCaslin.

    ISBN 1-55380-003-6

    I. Title.
PS8575.C43F57 2003   C811'.54   C2002-911117-X
PR9299.3.M42368F57 2003

At Ronsdale Press we are committed to protecting the environment. To this end we are working with Markets Initiative (www.oldgrowthfree.com) and printers to phase out our use of paper produced from ancient forests. This book is one step towards that goal.

Printed in Canada by AGMV Marquis

CONTENTS

ACKNOWLEDGEMENTS

Some of these poems appeared previously in *Prism international, Descant, The Fiddlehead, Acta Victoriana, Afterthoughts, White Wall Review, Queen's Quarterly, Room of One's Own, Vox Feminarum, Tickled by Thunder, The Best of Tickled by Thunder, 1998, Windhover, Quarter Moon Quarterly, Cormorant, Iris, Jones AV, The Antigonish Review, Christianity and Literature, The Malahat Review, Canadian Literature, The New Orphic Review, Pottersfield Portfolio, Grain,* and *The Merton Seasonal.* "Grace Notes" was a finalist in the Sandburg-Livesay Anthology for 1999 and was published in *Waiting for You to Speak: The Winning Poems of the 1998 Sandburg-Livesay Anthology Contest* (Unfinished Monument Press, 1999). "The Loneliness of Jesus" was a finalist in the Sandburg-Livesay Anthology Contest for 1999 and appeared in *No Choice but to Trust* (Unfinished Monument Press, 2000). "Wilderness/Poetry" appeared in *The Wilderness Anthology,* published by Outlaw Editions (1999). "A Blank Slate" received honourable mention in the Burnaby Writers' Poetry Contest for 1998. "Among the Elders" was a finalist in the Burnaby Writers' Society Millennial Poetry Contest for 2000. "Those Who Make Poetry with Their Lives" won 2nd place in *Room of One's Own* Millennium Poetry Contest. An early version of "The Fit of Song" was a finalist in the 1999 Acorn-Rukeyser Chapbook Contest. "Black Owl" appeared in the anthology *Running Barefoot: Women Write the Land* (Rowan Books, 2001). "The Road to Emmaus" was the third-place winner in the Burnaby Writers's Poetry Contest for 2001. "The Loneliness of Jesus," "Elder Brother," "A Midrash on the Kingdom Prayer," and "An Invocation to God the Mother," appeared in the anthology *Poetry and Spiritual Practice* (The St. Thomas Poetry Series, 2002). "Gender Benders" appeared in the anthology *The Other Eye* (Far Field Press, 2002). "Partners" will appear in an upcoming chapbook from Leaf Press. "Bombs and Bread" was a finalist in the Burnaby Writers' Society 2002 Poetry Competition.

I would also like to thank the following for their generous editorial assistance with various stages of the manuscript: my husband Mark Haddock, Catherine Owen, David Zieroth, Hannah Main-van der Kamp, Mary Haddock, Janet Allwork, and the Douglas College Creative Writing Group.

for my friends
Celeste, Eileen, Hannah, Janet,
Sister Eileen, and Catherine

THE NAMES
OF GREEN

—

To enter there is to become unnameable.
(Thomas Merton, from "The Fall")

White Meditation

Begins as a humming behind the ear
a musical mood, dark listening.

Meaning thrums, circles, intends
toward us, tends us well.

Why bother to arrest
that unlovely, unlikely suspect

of a thought? I'm no cop.
Let it go by. All strictures die.

Loop your skittish will
to the wild horsewoman.

Lasso yourself to the subtle stars
which are not fixed, glued.

Drop the priest and magus,
become the hermitess

small, brown and peripheral,
an effective nobody

in rainforest or desert
an occasion for speech, or silence.

When the world speaks
try not to get in the way.

A Blank Slate

*Try to be a sheet of paper with
nothing on it.*
                    —Rumi

1

Step on the tiles in cold, bare feet.
Kiss the words flying.

Letters in the updraft whirl,
savour of some unsung alphabet.

2

Something rises to the top.
Again, the poem is writing itself
with or without you.

No more willing it.
You are a handful of cinnamon
flung in the pot,
a sprinkling of yeast in the dough.

3

Exhale yourself in a breath of steam.
Inhale the world at your door:
fresh February snows on Burke Mountain,
quilt of kisses drawn
over a slumbering child.

4

The world will always be larger
and you will die into it (late or soon)
peering from a kitchen window
where the white hawthorn
preps for its own Spring term.

5

Grant yourself one mantra of breath
deep in the lungs.
Fast-walk from the suburbs of the body
to the fringing hills.

Dogs in short sweaters are there before you
nursing within themselves
the buried howl.

6

Stepping into the fluorescent Safeway air,
buy peppers — green, red and yellow.

Bring them home, cross-section them,
feed them to your loved ones in salad or pasta.

Clean up.
Lay out your books and pens on the table.
Be consoled,
consumed by the blank page.

7

This body's music:
footprints of tiny sparrows'
fretwork in the hills.

8

Midnight, your head is on the lap of the beloved.
The beloved knows
you are only pretending to be asleep,
listening to that breath
rising, falling.

Young Lake: Transformer

We are clouds passing into
the depths of your attention,
into each other and on,

kin of your pewter flesh
hurled from the flying dock
into open-book stars.

We are adroit with cries of loons,
sky-drinking eyes,
resurfacing as

woman-with-head-of-doe
man-with-velvet-antlers.

Cariboo Rain

With signs of dryness everywhere —
incense air
scrawny lodge pole pines dripping needles
and erect brown-topped firs,

the two-week rain comes as a boon
forcing us to the cabin
to stretch and catnap
and walk out at last
after a week of doing nothing

into the ruby gloss of rosehips
spread across the road,
the moony brown-eyed-Susans
and mauve daisies
tipsy in their twirl.

Release at Young Lake

A river quakes through aspen leaves
and my unhurried heart.

A train of mergansers chugs for shore;
eyes listen for minnows.

Cheeky chipmunks jabber and dart;
the chest rises and falls.

Aspiring osprey lifts, eagle dives;
a human brain undoes one knot.

Ants march under the door,
their core will burning.

The gliding loon releases its ghostly cry;
spirit cuts loose from the dock.

Every barefoot breath falls down
the blue, blue wind

down the paradise stair,
straight into the arms of fire.

Sometimes When Reading

eyes drop
off behind the print into void,
or, you could say, become aware of the print
as print and lose the drift of meaning
as it wafts ashen behind,
rising as plume or smoke signing
up for oblivion. I am
savage and illiterate,
wholly primitive;
the civilized Logos-world curls up
cuneiform, and scribe
of the abyss leans forward
groping to hear a pin fall,
continental drift of pages,
annunciation of some new
alphabet singing before the worlds.

Daddy Longlegs

Exquisite your six symmetrical legs
sprouting tiny prongs
your dun, air-brushed wings,
cherry-stem of a body —
brave camouflage.

Paused dancer
posing before me, all nerves.
Where is your slender and elegant tribe,
your sienna bride?

Lifting off from the desk lamp
you float like Ra in his boat of sun,
then batter madly across green glass,
freefall, slip behind my desk
and flee down a white corridor of wall.

Now there is only the sound of traffic
and a blank page to keep me company.

Silence to Wrap My Sleep Around

Something arises or is given,
grace in the mind and across the page

seabottle, something with echo of sea,
clear and subtle, caught in a sidelong glance.

Looked at the wrong way, it skitters off.
Heart heaves back in the chest.

Lyric incapacity to sustain the gift,
keep it up and moving.

Effort loses; attention brings it back
as silence wraps it round.

Out of that sleep, what linens,
beads and relicts fall?

Unwrapped, rapt,
wiser than snow.

Less a eureka moment
than a white flutter behind the ear.

The Fearful Shall Not Enter

The angel's first words are always,
Fear not, fear not, Mary.

And in the holy now kingdom
no fear mongers or anxious ones,

not because anyone is excluded,
but since fear casts us from our deep selves.

Most of our lives a fending off of phantoms
who, if they come, are not as they seem.

How many dreams a prospect of emptying,
falling, waking out of terror?

How many deaths a passport to somewhere
unimagined?

Meditation on Death: Arbutus Drive

The heart fingers its goblet.
An oak chair is drawn to a table
where apples blush in a blue bowl.

Gnarled arbutus puzzles the air.
Wheat-grass sifts its warmth
into lichen-covered rocks.

Ocean rolls on one vast side
where tilted clouds amass.
The gates of eye, ear, nose and mouth

shut down. Another tide rushes in
with unexpected calm.

The Dying Man Enters the Room

for Grace Hodgson

where his colleagues are gathered
over the business of poetry, and gives
the room a dignity they had not noticed it lacked
until he trod the soft shaft
of late afternoon sun slanting
through the window.

The dying man's face is swollen
but his eyes are as they had been
before the treatments, and he jokes
in the old way, telling of his wife's cares,
his daughter's jazz dance,
his son's progress at the university.

And they all know they too are dying,
but that the dying man has already
crossed to the extravagant light
and has chosen to grace them
in these hours before his death
with the undivided presence of his attention.

The Loneliness of Jesus

What we all want is a mind of journeys
weathered and wise, one
that has surpassed the grumble of days,
cupped in a primordial body.

Give me conifer breath in hazel eyes,
an apronful of apples, spilt seeds
shining, sliding on the floor.

The first to wander freely this world's halls
entered once in an upper room
in full humanity blazing.

Yet when the presence forms
in the matron with her cold sore,
the one-legged athlete,
or the foul-breathed dog,
few spring to meet it there.

How then he must hunger
for our windfall coming on the road.
How his emptied mind
must gape and yearn
to be among us fast and finally.

Elder Brother

Jesus, who could bear to be you,
carving out centuries with your metaphors —

buried pearls, cryptic, enigmatic tales,
your ragtag band of fishermen and thieves?

Little you care whether we remember you
as human or God. All that prickly disputation.

Your kingdom is still a child,
something lost and found.

Non-violent, yet such a guerrilla
you got yourself killed,

knew what that flattening death meant,
a showdown on a field, a sign.

To live like a field lily, springing back —
a few have done it.

The Road to Emmaus

If one doesn't know how to die, then he
doesn't know how to live either.
　　　　　　　　　　—Thich Nhat Hanh

One day, whether you are present or absent,
someone you love dies, taking a different
channel of the river or just skirting off
across the universe on skis.

Someone falls over the edge of a building
or lifts a skyward hand in a particular gesture
that flicks across the brow for the last time.
No arch remark, no instructions for burial.

A brother, father, mother or friend
who makes your heart burn within you,
right in the middle of ordinary tea and cakes
goes without end to the finale

leaving no lists of hymns or words for recitation.
This time the departure is so gradual
you miss its halt measure, tread
too gentle to be recognized as loss.

A person may be still alive before your eyes
but mentally away on some final pilgrimage,
as when my queenly mother's wrack
lay abstractedly on the institutional bed.

Fire flecked her eye then, and for a moment
the old wit returned. For a millisecond
she no longer confused me with her childhood friend.
One day, when you are halfway present

or going through the same stunts
like an acrobat through a gelatinous sea
someone you loved who was denied
will return and dance before your chambered eyes.

A Midrash on the Kingdom Prayer

better known as the *Lord's Prayer*
or the *Our Father.* It obviously addresses

someone more affectionate than a storm god,
someone more like the parent who listened.

The Kingdom Prayer is not about a kingdom.
It is about a presence on the lawn,

a prayer of the balancing of rhythms,
what we hear and what we don't hear.

Heaven is within, invisible, while
the Name is expressed, pressed out.

These are both true, as if to say,
holy what we see, holy what we don't see.

Then we get to forgiveness or reciprocity.
Everything forgiving everything is the kingdom.

It has no head of state.
Lead us not into temptation and *deliver us* are one.

There are always the holes to step into,
the scramble, and the helpers.

The delivering is active, like birth.
The kingdom is a child's kite winding in.

All you have to do is imagine it
and here it is. This presence now.

Liberation

(on a painting by F.H. Varley)

A man can embody truth
but he cannot know it.
                    —W.B. Yeats

Here, in the hive of our days,
you have left us an open door,
someone walking out of light
so dazzled it breaks to blue-green rose.

Matter too has changed
and the possibilities of flesh,
flayed, splayed, now
like an open palm, unnailed.

Here, now, we are that person
walking in, that being
walked into, a presence
in the part that vivifies.

Someone has entered
and overleapt the self to return
and say with all colours:
this body, it is good

as we glide through the door
to ourselves where honey globes,
dripping like streaks of paint
onto our hands, feet, tongues.

In this place and this crowning,
the box we once thought large enough
has broken like a lime sarcophagus.
We are liminal and literal and walking.

Wedding the Significant Other

Eye to blade with a patch of grass,
perched at its low height,
I am peaced.

But green words on amethyst air
are other than expected:

Wordy one, braceleted and wan,
not for tools, art or manuscripts
is your race known here,
but for separating yourself further
than any other.

I meet you at the Mercy Seat,
support you on a far strand of burgeoning land.

O naked ones,
you who have become your own tools.

Let the Green, Green Grass
Be Your Epicentre

says the Muse, who even for a woman
is a woman who wakes you up

in the middle of the night, dropping off
phrases like candy, then leaves you

to drag your own dreary weight.
Wait, she says, know your boundaries,

but always be open to boundlessness.
Surrender, she says, then says it again,

in case you didn't get the message the first time.
This is hard work, you think. Like breathing.

Then a sudden rupturing of the fabric —
jagged edge of raw blue silk torn from its skein.

Here, mid-pilgrimage, you pause,
not expecting anything in the drift.

She sits cross-legged on the ledge and says,
Let the green, green grass be your epicentre.

Panorama Ridge

Lush tangle of wet cedar bones,
moist embrace of licking ferns,

graceful, up to our heads,
rippling heat through nine kilometers

of switchbacks high to succulent
alpine meadows where we couple

under blue stars. Our breaths conspire
against mosquitoes and black flies

bouncing like raindrops on a pup tent
made for one. Eighteen years ago

we bonded in a tent. Now rejoining,
our tongues sing a bush fire,

quenched by lupine, heal-all, fireweed
blown anemone, white heather,

and the mild rein orchid.
We are brown marmots, camouflaged,

khaki lovers anointing our lost, found flesh
for the steep descent, and long glissade home.

Partners

When your dear eyes first lit on mine
an unseen scapular wrapped me round.

"Hippyish," twenty-seven, celibate,
I deemed you raw, mere student of eighteen.

Years later at the university our talks
became an exchanging of small white stones.

Then at the lake, I saw your burnished face
ripen before me. I became your circular moon,

wishing in my womb a child could wander
to cast herself an exile to the world.

Nothing pure brings total ease:
some tumult, sulks, criticism, walls.

Our walks became hurried strolls
for three through desert malls.

Yet here we lie after twenty years
in this unearned, elegant hotel,

seasoned, unsullied, soft, all faces bare,
marked by the light like wild twin deer.

Encamped

Muir's stunning Yosemite is surrounded
by tourists jostling for camera positions.

Still we camp in a grove of ponderosa pines
whose lyric canopy becomes a marriage tent.

Breakthrough. Occluded stars drop
diamond earrings on the lobes of trees.

Our eyes turn from dusk's dimness
to sip the scarred and lovely Milky Way.

Old and new testaments of love
sing streams of psalmody across the sky.

El Capitan, Half Dome, Sentinal
and other half-cracked lovers,

flung like erratics, monumental,
create this stonescape for the duration:

evenings, days, centuries, millennia.
Somehow our littleness is included

even with the swarms
gawking at paradise.

At Sooke Basin

Your forehead should not be tense at all . . .
　　　　　　　　　　　　— The Kabbalah

1

An endearing circular beast curls into itself like a nautilus.
Mercurial light filters through the *corpus callosum*

bridging the two firmaments of the brain.
Intertidal fingers loosen, shake out in slow folds.

Neck stretches, arms and legs flex.
The small enduring beast is a she thing,

something flicking its tail through the sea.
Next time she will awake further inland as a rainforest

with cool dripping brow and maidenhair ferns.

2

Black-and-white moths kiss this faithful shore.
Sun slowly massages the baroque curtains of the brain

kneading its cake-batter convolutions.
Garry oaks, jocund crones, toss off their hats.

I am here to untie some gnarling in myself.
What do I want? Total annihilation? A new face?

No. Just a clean line running straight out to sea.

3

A rakish merganser and his dowdy mate
slide into view. He tosses his crest high.

Serrated beak carves letters in a gray sea.
Happily, my own brilliant-plumaged mate

is away with our offspring who needs me
less and less each day. I must do now

what God does in the beginning —
withdraw — clear a space, make

a caesura in time. Let her struggles draw her
by her inward tides, and find my own.

A few sparks now, *scintilla animae*,
remain hidden in things.

Diamonds, for instance, dripping
from Mrs. Merganser's back.

4

I sleep till noon, let dishes pile
like shipwrecks in the sink,

slop around in coat and pajamas all day;
sip white wine and giggle with my friend.

Dawn. Enormous pillars of white fog
hewn out of ether. Dusk. Mrs. Merganser

drifts past my window in vestments of trim brown.
A double rainbow signs the font of shore.

Contemplation

Accustomed to distraction
somehow I fell into a sacred space,
template awaiting its musical score
(myself devoid of music).

A robin in the rain
could have told me
in the streaked gray
all was silent.

Water splashed in a pond
like words around their hush.

For Thomas Merton

1

You in your Kentucky woods with the deer.
I wrapped up here in a ring of cedars,

moss greening my bones, the droop
of maidenhair fern and misted sword fern

yawning an innocent mist into my brain,
a single jay skimming away for the ravine.

In all this relentless wetness
something says the world is water,

something says silence holds
and hides its lush cascades.

May the fire that wed you
be my first date and my last sentence.

2

You entered a longing for all things
obscure, silent and brief.

Your prodigal tongue still wrests
flame from desert air.

With you in dark I thrive:
cenobite, solitary, hermit, activist.

3

With soles of your feet still wet,
you were leavened
into the absurdity of your good death.

Socrates gave a discourse
then quaffed his hemlock.

You only spoke of disappearing
and the need for a quick coke.

Yet disciples gathered.
And when you found you were at last
for your calling
wild enough
you thunderbolted into the mountain's
other side.

4

In your journals you punctuate your sentences
with birds — lark, ptarmigan, wren,

so when I step into the hot pastiche of your words
I glimpse slantwise from margins

your uninterrupted, heavenward thrust,
uncorrected as the flight of birds.

How my morning entries brighten in your light
and Protestant lists ache for your falling cables.

Voluble man of silence, no ghost, intervene
between my grief and your breviary of days.

Into the Whirlwind

How long till the woman of sorrows enters the whirlwind of the
striped tulip, whirlwind of the hummingbird's wing? How long
till she lodges between the redwood's bark and its sap, till a
woman of no blame dances where Leviathan and Behe-
moth are two prongs of one dilemma, plunging deep-
er into the oven of bliss where God wrestles herself
for a blessing suffering beside us inside the
wronged tree through a tornado of bliss
and bane then blazing in the dark
whooshing spiral of the peacock's
eye or in the chittering chim-
panzee dark? How long till
the saint is spit from
the dragon's eye
and the seed
lets itself
fall

open,
till the
engorged
sky empties its
wealth of rain on
the prophet's wind-
stirred head? How long
till the Magdalen undoes her
hair and Christ blazes in the sev-
ered amoeba brain? How long till the
toes and fingers trace riddling words, till
the books fling out their stories of healing and
the nesting tables of the soul set out the only food.
How long till God's entering Job is Job's entering God,
till periphery and centre merge again till the closed cubicles
release their honey and the wild wolves play tug-of-war in gentleness?

Christ Meets Eve in the Underworld

The harrowing road he runs along
leads him at last to wetland greenery
drenched in a lifeless hail of gray,
where she, our first Mother, clothed
in a dress of pomegranate flame
scrapes away the moss and leaves
that stop an underground stream.

Her eyes, lighting on the tall stranger,
brim tears at his words: *Ave, Eva* —
greeting material, germane.
She scoops some water into a ladle
and lifts it to his lips: *How is it you come
so late to this dim vestry, dragging
words as from a lost domain?*

*Depth of Earth, you who took the blame
before the loss of paradise,
take from me now this massive crucifix
and let me bend my will to yours
releasing all your wilderness
into the mechanical cities.*

Together they weave a spiritual body,
cut a window in the forehead
for the oasis of visions,
and set a door-harp in the cavity
where once an ailing heart had lain.
Through the mouths of creatures
flies the immaculate Jesus-Mother

skimming into the world she never left behind.

The Omnipresence of Moss

The Cauldron Mother rolled it from her apron
patting it into a damp, spongy ball,
then laid it among triads of hemlock, cedar, fir,
flinging it last of all into the orbit of Neptune

where it magnified itself in unstoppable green,
tufting and clustering in decay,
cryptogamous, keeping from everyone
the spores of its hidden marriage.

Had the Mother chosen Mars, that armed
red planet might have renounced war
and all its trouble, for green carries
such softness to the eyes.

Even in this westcoast neighbourhood
no herbicide can keep it from wrapping itself
around tree trunks, stones and the crevices
of my misty March garden.

Again and again it lowers itself to places
below our feet, offering itself to weary heads
in all its myriad shades of green
and in all the drenched names of green.

All I would ask now is a chaise longue of mosses,
just for a few moments to be pavillioned
close as stone to moss.

OB-LA-DI-BLA-DA

(Life in the Burbs)

—

If you want some fun,
sing Ob-la-di-bla-da
— The Beatles

Grace Notes

1

you are my going to myself to gather myself
home

2

how your spine curves against mine
when we huddle in

arranging what we know
around what centre

How we feel the workings
of each in each

the muscled speech
and slackening into sleep

3

if there is no spirit we can name
still, all our bright language will return —
dew on our heads

if language is a construct, conduit,
what of that?

4

sometimes the companion is the beloved
and sometimes the beloved is a
sharer of tasks

harnessed there,
you glance at each other
through blinders

remembered meadows

5

often we are too tired, numb,
to turn to each other

almost lost, the desire
that otherwise might come flaring

6

there is always the possibility:
one of us lank-haired,
vomiting bile

one finding the pressure points
on the other's spine,

one hooked up to tubes,
the other waiting
in a close room

7

or I holding your unmuscled flesh
guiding you toward the shower

o love, let us be true

all the pieces falling around us
and the cries of blue horses

when you are old and grey and full of sleep

8

in your first vision of me
I floated toward you, veiled —
you naked as Adam

who will go first
all passions blown
still hungering

and who will linger,
o, my second skin,
face within my face?

Crossing the Street

Traffic light signals *go go*
while on the wire a busy jay natters

fails to be drawn into the net
of the walker's elliptical brain

which soon notes his patient
leanings into light,

the a cappella solo, flaunting crown.
wordflow is Godflow

but the jay holds luminosity,
now aiming for the nearby fir

a bowl of mosses and a mate.
Perhaps five hidden eggs. God knows.

Mine the slender words;
his the fulgent song.

A Flying Dream After
Ten Years' Grounding

How often I used to dream
the rotary buzz of wings,
small nubs tingling in my back
then the breaking
to tilt with planetary bodies.

Today I coast ungainly
as a pudgy goose at Como Lake
over the lift off, breathless,
feet dragging on the damasked rug.

Stumblingly
with a shoulder's wrench
down a long gallery
I gaze wistful through glass
practising what I have already forgotten.

Written on a Visa Receipt After
the Consumer's Fiftieth Birthday

Breaking out of the boxes
into somewhat larger boxes
she finds the suburban dreamhouse
has cradled her orderings and disorderings
for ten improbable years —

But now, suddenly
into the open at fifty,
she knows that if she does not risk it all,
risks will suddenly take her.

Cupid is back,
that flighty, naughty lad
who cares nothing for youth or age,
or even middle age.

Stolen Time

You take four or five deep breaths in the car's belly
because there are no more items on your list,

bewildered, peeled open, surprised
a space in your chest is humming.

Is it possible you are singing? Gratitude
pours into the scribbles of your day book.

Attention fails, slow downshift of gears.
Outside, a crow selects a single stone.

The face of your birth rises from your head.

Interruptions

Get used to them
as God does when She tends
to fry and fish, flipping from sea to shore
then settling in the interstices.

Be macaronic and diverse.
Let words and silences engrave your skull.
Be that narrow bone house
Then go outside

Stop complaining.
Be luxuriant as sky
in its sequined cry.
Be a white bone stripped by sun.

Give in. Once in a while
between this and that
a thrush will open
the slow perfumery of its throat.

Be mindful like one
who plays voluble
then dumb.

Feet Addressing Head

Hey dude, give us some space and turf,
you, rumbling up there
in your bright, abstract buzz.
You could go flying off, incapacitated
without us down here to keep you real,
you in your bulbous, bloodless dome.

Remember, we are your contact with ground zero.
Bathe us with myrrh and balm,
massage us once in a while
and maybe we will remember you
when the two of us lie tip to toe
partnered for the long journey home.

The Monster

You would not think a monster sleeps
under this agreeable facade
extending down layers and layers,
only disturbed by the slow
burndown of a long fuse.

Yet there is this crazed, genderless thing
that erupts once or twice a year,
bold enough to brandish a hairbrush
over a child's head,
to enjoy the terror in her eyes,
to shatter her recorder against a wall,
then sprawl downstairs in
an eerie three-block-scream
kicking all the time like a centipede against walls
mouthing her mother's old cliché,
You're driving me to the grave.

There are these two heads,
one barely attached to the other
by a piece of floss.
One quick, waxen snip
would send one flying.

Caliban

My soul longs to flow
into the tattered lace of tides,
but daily constraint,
this hogshead of shelter,
confines me in its cube.

I would utter forests.
Something there like God
does not loathe a sigh.

Stepping Out of My Skin

The skin slips to the floor
like a worn bear costume.
I am Marsyas flayed,
examining in the mirror

freshly exposed muscle,
tight new silken sheath.
I think about putting
new wine in the old skin,

but know it has to go.
This story is about shedding.
The ouroboros shaft
crinkles and hisses

in fire at my feet.
I have been drawn, perilous,
out of the head of the snake
and there is no going back.

Black Footlocker

I had almost forgotten the black footlocker
belonging to my father during the war,

its brass hasps and worn brown leather handle,
the fasteners on either side snapping into place,

the musk of its interior, a case for books,
a coffee table, a suitcase for innumerable moves;

how it disappeared one day never to return.
Did I throw it out, take it to the dump,

leave it out in the rain on garbage day?
I ache for its smooth innards,

its resting place for my feet,
the unnecessary weight of it,

covered with stamps as from a journey.

Fistfalls of Dark in the Suburbs

It is a lovely world
in your clean village of honeysuckle trellises,
aerobics centres and pet salons
except for the dehydrated woman
sleeping in a doorway near Hastings and Gore.

It is a winter paradise with delicate icicle lights
strung from the porch
except for the frozen child locked outside
your sliding glass door.

It is lovely and calm in your bunker
except for the fist-bitten dark
and bloodied, stigmated palms
about to shatter the peace of your aerodrome,
the wild dogs pressing their noses
against your plexiglass.

It is a small, small, wonderful world after all
except that your head is Siamese-twinned
to the head of a bagman and wet moths
shudder in the lights of your dream.

It is a fine prospect
except for the lean Christs
shadowing your well-exercised flesh
and the starvation whispers of anorexic children.

Those Who Make Poetry with Their Lives

for J.A.

Some listen more than talk, moving
with quiet grace through our lives,
joining choirs rather than taking private vocal lessons.

Would to God that all the Lord's people were prophets,
said Blake, meaning *artists,* but art expanded
to include all those anonymous acts
that smooth and oil the world
and move it to the fulcrum like a dancer.

Think of the unknown carvers of stone,
workers in stained glass
who would have called themselves
craftspeople, never asking to have their names
etched for all to see,

or people patiently teaching the minutiae of grammar,
and thought, glamour of the public body,
syntax of love, spoken
without too much fuss and bother

carefully editing the inaccurate and false
from the language that cups us,
quietly shaping policy for the *polis,*
effective transformers
working their own kind of brave magic,
carrying the elders and the young on their backs

so we can say what we mean
and speak what we speak with clarity
and ease, so our thoughts might be
sane and decent to the core.

Another Blakescape

I walk into the clanging streets
and see Blake's tygers raging there,
but no one else can spy them till
I comb them from my hair.

The lady in the lion suit,
the acrobats at the malls,
are doing mental somersaults
and cracking acorns on the walls.

The sunflowers are tittering
and angels turn their wayward heads,
the mad are out on holiday,
the rationalists sleeping in their beds.

Falling Asleep, Thinking of Blake Again

and all those rat-a-tat voices
from the other side of the wall.

Eternity too Greek a word
for so many rooms and windings.

Discourse leads to Socrates
chatting with his daimon,

and Dostoyevsky's voices.
How Blake's face must have wrinkled

up in a laugh when he first saw his section
in *The Norton Anthology of English Literature*

right up there with his heroes Spenser and Milton,
and all those Cambridged, titled ones,

and he impoverished autodidact
with his Cockney blast of vision.

Writing to Magnolia

When the big sag comes
I say to magnolia,
how satiny your leaves
and add to myself,
it really could be worse
than raking May magnolia petals
into fragrant heaps, delighting
in delicate mauve streaks,
seeing how easily they bruise
how much solitude they require,
how they are shaped like oblong pears.

(She wants what Yeats said woman could never have:
to be loved for herself alone
and not her yellow or auburn hair.)

That and more:
the mastery in love,
and you, Magnolia,
casting your fleshy dress
like snow at my feet.

Dear Prime,

You told me your name directly when I found you on our driveway — *Prime*, as in *Robin redbreast in his prime*, and *prime*, because you gave me the gift of your death on the second liturgical hour and because, though you were common, part of the common longing for spring, you were first and original to me. I held your stillness in my breath, then moved my fingers into your breast, so recently puffed full blown. You were warm but your small neck was broken. You must have plunged into the window of the truck where later I found a few of your casual feathers, and died with no sound but that one dull thud. I wrapped you in a towel, brought you to the sink (no flap or flutter), and closed your enameled eyes, noticing the colour of your breast was rust, burnt orange, not red at all. The tiny feathers bunched back finely along your neck, made you seem larger than you were, your feet curled away in the stillness of deep meditation. I buried you near the irises in the garden.

Chiasmus

To our pet rat Casper, put to sleep July 31, 1999

Because you were too afraid to step,
too faint to go, we helped you
to the tidiness of death

then placed your bones in a small box
sensing you would rather spring this cage
than drag paralyzed feet behind.

Now you are curled away from your cancer.
A child has decked you with hollyhocks,
nibbles of cheese, folded notes and poems.

She would have me touch the silk of your lids,
and I do, but at her age could not gaze
into the open coffin of my aunt

or at forty view my father's waste.
So late I double back to wake
into the full rotunda of your eye

shy grace captive all its days,
though in the wild, death would have come
cleaner than from our ceremonial hands.

Two Scenarios

1

Casper the friendly rat
lived to ninety in rat years
stroked and fondled
in her neat fawn coat,
winning the SPCA best habitat award.

On the day of her funeral
flowers were placed in rows,
notes written, poems uttered
to honour the *world's best rat.*

From her a family learned gentleness.

2

Lab rat 492, also born captive
was force-fed 1000 mgs. of vitamin C
by mouth twice daily at 12-hour intervals
for a period of three weeks.

Stress was produced daily
by one hour of complete
physical restraint
in a wire mesh cylinder cage.

Randomly, during the immobilization,
the rat was placed in a head-down
position for fifteen minutes.
Then they killed the rat

and looked at his adrenal glands
which, amazingly,
produced more stress hormones
than in rats not subjected to the test.

Now, happily, a family knows to take its vitamin C.

Miranda

I dreamt I gave birth to a small deaf mute
whose name was clearly Miranda
because she looked and looked
but made no cry or moan slipping
from the glossy pink canal into the world
where the doctor marked her chart FLB
(funny looking baby) and would not offer
a word to calm my deep alarm

though how like the ancient Sarah
I laughed when told the joke
of my burgeoning mid-life womb
knowing I would love this slip
of a girl so longed for
so silent in her wild gaze

Aphorisms for the Addicted

1

In the land of the lists
      a far cry from the holy Presence,
The *jihad* is for breath,
      a spaciousness.

2

Fighting to please customers:
      not a good model for education.

3

Spending every moment figuring how to maintain balance,
      one tumbles off the treadmill.
            Happy fall.

4

Running as fast as you can to stay in the same place:
      that Oxford don Lewis Carroll said it all.

5

Bring back the commas and semicolons:
      slow the pace of the sentence.

6

Pace of our lives:
       unsustainable as our logging practices.

7

God never busts her butt;
       yet everything gets done.

Black Owl

I find you on the path,
flaccid mass of feather and bone,
cat ears laid back against your head,
eyes like wild broom, centres of daisies.

Your right wing is dusky as a raven's,
drooped like a broken wishbone,
so I thrust you halfway into my overcoat
and walk the long mile to the wildlife refuge
praying all the zigzag way
into your luminous eyes.

To the Buddhas of Bamiyan in
the Hillside Cliffs of Afghanistan

now blasted, bested by man to kingdom come.
Your obituaries were short-lived in the free press.

The hands that carved you out of a cliff's rib
now draw you back into a pummeled dark.

Pilgrims who studied the largesse of your lids
have passed on, though one sorry grey pigeon,

plummeting past your leveled bones,
rested briefly on a hummock of dirt.

Gaping caves swallowed you whole.
Gypsy moths of your dust sprinkled all who kissed

ground zero at your no longer present feet.
All your noble truths are shucked,

all that suffers you enter again.
The ground itself seems homeless now.

Bombs and Bread

God sent manna, Allah sent Gabriel;
we send grim parcels of doom —
bombs with bread — for good measure,
pressed down, little futile loaves.

How will the woman with her shattered son
in her arms, that Mary, Fatima,
digest the bitter bread, or pass
its incinerated crusts to her remaining child?

"Collateral damage" visited on one innocent
rationalized by the death of ten terrorists.
Cold math, ignoring the central text:
"Love your enemies. Do good to those who hate."

The canons of this world think Jesus naïve,
honouring him in churches, not the field.
Bombers roar, terror fragments
into the veins of the body politic.

Nowhere do muddied troops melt down their guns.
Smart bombs, not seeds, are planted in the earth.
Jesus continues praying in Gethsemane,
telling Peter to sheathe his sword.

and again is lifted on the bloodied cross,
head drops to chest — the sabachthani cry,
while in deserts and towns the clever human apes
close hearts and sound the drum.

Composition by Field

Love is more a listening than an observing,
phrases grown in the laboratory of the ear.

Not field notes or a painterly eye,
though the ear has its azure strokes.

A subtle attunement — like osprey and shore —
with the stress on melody, *melos.*

When the disrupter earthquakes into my life
how will I welcome her requiem?

When the fishes fall out of the boat
and the silent fisher goes home hungry

who will catch in the whorl of the ear
the last rays of light?

MATRILINEAL
LINES

—

*This cathexis between mother and daughter — essential,
distorted, misused, is the great unwritten story.*

*Until a strong line of love, confirmation,
and example stretches from mother to daughter, from
woman to woman across the generations,
women will still be wandering in the wilderness.*

— Adrienne Rich (from *Of Woman Born*)

An Invocation to God the Mother

for Julian of Norwich

Bless us

God the holocaust mother
God the harried housekeeping mother
God the multi-tasking mother
God the mother of anorexic girls
God the singed mother of furnaces
God the mother subsisting on beans
God the mother typing God knows what
God the poet mother
God the engineer mother
God the weeping mother
God the fatigued mother
God the wild and sequined mother
God the sweet mother napping
God the crosswise mother dancing
God the resurrected mother singing opera
God the born-again mother in the stables of suburbia
God the Messiah mother
God the mother saying Kaddish for her mother
God the babbling, pellucid grandmother
God the foreshortened mother
God the motherless mother
God the untamed hyena mother
God the designing mother of looms and tapestries
God the intertidal mother with anemones and starfish
    in her hair
God the lioness mother in her pride

Bless us

New Earth

a brown woman with finches
in her dense tangle of hair,

cloak of sage mosses on her shoulders,
circlet of twigs for a headdress

threaded with deer fern,
feet wrapped in alder leaves

body caressed by yards of new snow.
If you wait in first light you will glimpse her

hanging a cluster of magenta berries
on the wild mountain ash by the fence.

Soon the russet thrush and her mate
will pounce, dash the clumped snow

from the branches into the snowpack.
How deftly her hands all the while

soften the sod with the plowing hours,
as she dreams spring in the deep underground.

The Pause

Hooded owl, horned and snowy owl
of ripened, ringed eyes,
grey Arctic wolf in hullabaloo,
Canada goose on warmed nest,
grub and masticating beetle,
amoebae in wavering dance,
subatomic particle in wave's sonata,
eight-year-old girl in leggings
pounding a western beach:

let all the earth keep silence.

Conch

In one of the White Rock shops
it stood out as something
entirely non-native, exotic,
suggesting Caribbean sunsets.

Ten years from marriage and a child
I scooped it for she-who-would-perhaps-someday-emerge
a daughter in a pink room
with starlight wallpaper and acrobatic puppets

and if not for her then I'd buy it for me —
child-who-is-still-lost
looking for a pink boudoir where she
can sit at her own desk and write

whatever she wants
even words leading past the paperweight shell
into more shadowy mansions
the original creature left behind.

Interior Castle

A child crawls in play
up the tractionless, pink slide of the conch,
up to its first chamber,
but slides back down like Sisyphus' stone

then slowly regains the first terrace,
a room so ample it riffles light.

Some soft creature has smoothed the floor,
leaving its sheen,
and on the roof, a turret
of brittle spikes.

A Word for Those Who Come After

If you choose to enter this family
of pioneers, farmers, preachers, teachers, artists —
give time no forethought,
neither the riches of criticism,
nor the spoils of neglect.

Bring forgiveness like water in your hands.
Let it flow down, an oblation
on the whole house.

If you tread the ramshackle boards
of this stage, wear velvet and lace
or strip yourself like St. Francis to the nub.

Defy the crazies, bizarre juxtapositions
of too much praise, too little
cupping of the soul.

Be prepared to bear yourself over the threshold,
make your way in an alien world.

Though your enemies be those of your own household,
forgive them,
leave them with a shaking of the dust,
a quiet shalom.

Blessed Are the Poor in Spirit

In some livable future
I will walk in on my brave
girlself, trying to be perfect.

She is twelve and playing alone in her room
with an early prototype of Barbie
cutting paper dolls with red and blonde
long straight hair, perfect tiny waists.

She is too old for this game
so the room is locked. She is reading
her mother's guide to becoming a woman
and her period has not come; she is behind
all her friends. She has tons of homework
and will turn to it soon
for she wants perfect grades,
so she lies in her bed memorizing
the names and dates under the pictures
though she has a headache and
has just swallowed too many aspirin.

I shall hold her hands and look into her eyes
saying, *There is no Prince Charming*.
You are beautiful without drudgery
and meant to be queenly
but more than doll, consort or queen mother.
Stones and stories are mixing in your blood
and you are sorting them, you are
Rapunzel leaving her tower
to meet herself in the glen.

You are writing yourself and the stories
of women, and poems are bounding out of closets
and file drawers and people care.
You are about something I cannot see.
You are Lady Poverty because you have risked
everything and remained yourself.
You are living off the wages of light
which is feast, and the kingdom
is laid out before your arms, fingers, lips.
What you want is already spread before you
and you do not know it.

Aunt Josie's Cameo

They whispered she fell in love with a soldier,
gave him her wild, immaculate heart, became engaged.
Then, without telling her, he married a nurse during the war.

They said she refused to wed ever,
or even look at someone else all those long years,
becoming that slighted paragon, the old maid.

When I knew her at ten, she was plump, warm,
a fine Southern cook and nurturer of four strapping brothers,
her house the manse in Alabama where
all the relatives flocked like rotund
turkeys for Thanksgiving and Christmas.

She was a business success,
a woman with her own dress shop,
importing fashions from New York,
who made her living answering to no male whim.

But now, all of her I own rests
in this ivory cameo with its smooth-skinned
lady's face, demi-roses in her coiffed hair,
the bone of her fibre, worked gold
fallen into my palm,

carried on lapel or tucked under chin
through my twenties
for her enduring fortitude,
my fiction of her secret grief.

The Old, Beginning

Décolletage of mountains in spring,
the naked arbutus, and now

these old ones bathing.
Who can delineate their desire?

Even the dilapidated
lure night wind to their faces.

Even the shattered image of the decoy
desires love, not liquidation.

Chide me, dear stone
for stale breath and gnarled teeth.

Faith, Hope and Charity
but the greatest of these is Charity.

Phantasms plant plantations
in dimming brain's declivity.

Floor after factory floor,
a slow collapse of lights.

Pilgrims parade in walkers past
night stations of the cross.

Wit and wisdom salt
the rough word salad they toss.

Egyptian embalmers siphoned out
the worthless brains

but wrapped the endless heart in gold.

Petrified at Every Turn

From wheelchair row the view can be grim.
You swallow the horse pill of the world sitting down.

A whiskey's what I mostly need,
she said, cryptic, bemused.

This is finally the loosening of words
as when a child is everything

before all divisions and theories. Nothing
matters now but the whispered transmissions.

The eye is the same, mandala of the eye.
Cat tiptoes by, sentient, unconcerned.

These are the proverbs of Phyllis
At Crossroads Retirement Center:

Watch your words. Never
Put your faith in a sphinx.

Beware of chocolates.
Sometimes they shoot bolts of electricity

that blunder about the room.
Don't worry about me

I'm sitting in the Mercy Seat.

Two Voices

My peach origami tulips
cut and folded for Mother's day
lie in the garbage where you, mother,
left them a year later
to make way for something new.
I felt like a discarded blossom.

Daughter, how I cast my eyes over
slightly tatty paper flowers,
thinking to clear the decks,
that you'd not notice or care.

But the boil of rage on your artisan face
told me otherwise, drawing forth too late
my useless apology.

Still we plucked them, mother,
from coffee grounds and carrot peels
and you helped me mend the stem
with tape and glue, placed them back
in the rose vase on the piano.

And I forgave you
as children often do.

Protecting the Artist

Carve her room in jade
for she is only eleven but sophisticated
in her argument for writing late into the night
on pale leaves the snippets that come
tumbling in the inbetween
of school, lessons and homework.

At eleven o'clock in the evening
when she should be drifting over Florence
in a cloud of Botticelli light
or calling to children under the Ponte Vecchio,
she is wailing again because there is no time
to paint the unravelling seams of her bear,
her grandmother's yellow wood violets.

Carve her room in amber
for she is only eleven and hates her life
when she bends to the desires of others
instead of writing chapter three of the story
about a boy who lost his house
but fell into a conflagration so bright
it changed his nerdy friend into a hero.

Carve her room in rose quartz
when she is teased the next day at school
for charcoal smudges under her eyes
and recite into your flesh the lyrics
hid under her bed, her smothered singing.

On My Daughter's Twelfth Birthday

After the pizza joint and bowling,
I rake the leaves of the magnolia
which has cast its milky coat.

What can I wish to mark this rite
but that, as she is passing beautiful,
she may not rue her life.

A Two-Day Escape from Dullsville

Volunteering to go into a volley
of pre-pubescent hormones
at kids camp where nubile bodies
glow in the dark, small breasts bud

I confiscated all the flashlights,
squawking at the girls till eagles came
in the morning, drowning my voice.
Now I am vanishing into a dot

on the Thetis Island ferry
watching your friends towed
in tubes near the dock, thinking
the zodiac of stars a child of twelve

with some compartments filled,
your hands, mauve starfish gripping down,
your fists, hot pink peony buds
about to admit a world of ants.

For you at twelve, anything is possible,
your taste buds large as dragon's
at the back of your mouth.
You are balancing sun and moon

like marbles in a whirligig,
becoming a person I never
could have imagined. My love
fiercest in these partings.

Juice

These pre-pubescent girls in my back seat
are warm syrup. Honey wells from their pores,

sweat streams down their backs,
winding through the soft down of underarms.

They are virgin maples fluxed with sap,
foreheads, studies in pulchritude,

honeysuckle breath misting
my rear view mirror as they stretch

languorous toes curled under lean legs.
They dream long-haired boys with drums.

Such sweet, sprawling animals.
Tears spill so easily from transparent lids.

Heraclitus says, *The dry soul is wisest and best,*
but I wonder. What mother wrapped

in her sere autumn leaf would not steal
just one vial of that juice?

Knots

She says she is a worry to herself,
a series of knots, one springing up
just where another was undone,
Gordian, unyielding,

her agile fingers troubling themselves
all day, sometimes prematurely elated,
then falling back to task —
child labour of the soul.

She is my flesh, my dream,
but her knots have grown full size.
I thank her for the metaphor —
my life too a tensed cord

at which I pluck and pluck.
What are her dense ligatures?
Homework, exclusions, indifferent boys,
a mind that picks at gravel with the birds?

Who, having survived one adolescence,
would take to it again? Who
can learn from anyone else's rope tricks
those cool sleights of hand?

Gender Benders

My daughter and her cousin glide
in their superfluous sports bras

but today they masquerade as boys,
trying out the swagger and strut,

baseball caps reversed, chains
dangling from invisible wallets.

Hey dude, check this out!
issues in pseudo baritone.

They swat at wasps
(You're dead, man!)

striding free and confident
where yesterday they ran screaming.

Now in their king-of-the-barnyard way
they play a rough parody

of boys, the taut, tearless bodies,
cocksure construct that divides.

Advocate

How many times . . . I have wished that I could, even
if for a few short moments, look out into the world
through the eyes with the mind of a chimpanzee.
                                            —Jane Goodall

Like Jane, that White Ape born with a difference,
you wore your play bear hairless from love,

hyper sensitive to what a dog, cat, rat,
might feel beneath its skin,

exquisitely disturbed by any hint
of whip, goad, maze, unable

to read *Black Beauty* without rage.
At five, you ran shrieking from the cinema

at even a disneyfied version of human cruelty —
eggs dripping from the blank,

bland, all absorbing face of Quasimodo.
Studying trophy heads mounted in a lodge,

you declared yourself forever vegetarian at eight
and stuck to it, as if your parents' pates

had dangled there in numb suspense.
Cruelty is the worst of human sins,

wrote Jane in her autobiography.
So you would be Poet Laureate of beasts.

If in a dream, Flo, the compassionate
chimpanzee mother, were to take your hand,

you would not draw it back
for all their brutal wars

but look steadily from her pithy eyes
to their arboreal world.

Among the Elders

Here you stand at twelve
conversing among your elders,
astonishing precocity and power —
breathless parents barely
catching up to see you
slipping across a threshold.

Say, just for the sake of argument,
like that Jewish kid of long ago
you could stand in the full
integrity of your voice,
all the envious adult world poised
for the announcement of some godly business.

Let's say twelve is a breakthrough —
stature, grace, holy scrolls unrolling
from one hand, the other clutching
lip gloss, nail polish, gel,
teen magazines and angst.
This precipice, you say,
no business of ours.

Sonnet from a Stranger

Out of my mother's womb, that kindred space,
I groped onto this reef some years ago.
In me, she coined no replica of her face,
bearing a female other's quieter glow.
Today, at fifty-five, I stroke her hands,
veins crisscrossed under parchment there on loan.
No worries about managing her lands,
her substance gone to lawyers, nursing home.
Befuddled, slowly sucking on her thumb,
she bears my ministrations like a child.
I chatter on, though even the light is dumb,
hoping to glimpse her undefeated wild.
How strange, she suckles me in this dim shade,
where yet time's deep alliances are made.

Heaven Tree
(Carmanah Valley, Vancouver Island)

Fungus climbs your steep side,
lilies cling to the hem of your skirt,
needles extend into the moist air.
Your bole is throne and seat
for many invisible parasites

All feed on you
but you never complain
of their dependency,
being drained, having to sustain
the whole thing in midair

Take, eat —
this is my body
green and brown and unbroken,
broken
for you

Wilderness/Poetry

The wild deer wandering here and there
Keep the human soul from care.
— William Blake

Like all good mothers
she takes time out
in her remote house of cedar.

There is a syllabus we cannot master
        and it has no name.

A burning bush of bright florets.

Once we hiked into an alertness
        of alpine air: showers of quickened lupine
met our gaze, steadily cupping
        and releasing gold pollen
                too small for touch.

Even when the marmots almost
        played pet for us
begging for biscuits, we knew
        we were a matter of indifference
                wholly peripheral

and it is good to be dethroned,
        not to be chief priest in the middle
                of the apocalypse
with God the Father above, brutes
        and grass at heel. Here

the abyss is a roiling cauldron
            spewing up forms so lovely
                        they silence speech.

We are their metaphor,
            but for what? The presence
has changed before we can name it
            or say, *this,*
                        this is the meadow
where we wandered and expelled ourselves
            this kingdom opening at our feet —

fireweed, paintbrush,
            anemones recklessly imitating old men.

From this, we carved our box hedges
            and English country gardens.

What is the name for a microcosm of ivory
and white explosions contoured by tiny black bugs?

Queen Anne's lace? Not likely.
Unless you can imagine a million
neoclassical collars
handed out to the populace.

We have argued from design to deity,
but who can conceive a mind this
full of bones and ruminations?

In faith we call it love,
            and move to say how wilderness is like poetry
throwing off topiary sonnets,
            diving into *vers libre* to push
                        that order again into a disarray
implying closure
            but never closing. Wilderness

gulping solitude
      pausing in its own mirror
          of glacial ice
              cupped by undulations of mountains —
    anaphora down a page
chooses the fragile image, lean line of pine along a ridge

intuits and digresses,
     stands witness to itself
        in bright caesuras

           where we fall into language.

ABOUT THE AUTHOR

SUSAN McCASLIN was born in Indianapolis, Indiana and immigrated to Canada in 1969 to do graduate work in English at Simon Fraser University. She has been a Canadian citizen since 1977 and has taught English at Douglas College in New Westminster, B.C. since 1984. Susan has published six volumes of poetry and edited the anthologies *A Matter of Spirit: Recovery of the Sacred in Contemporary Canadian Poetry* and *Poetry and Spiritual Practice*. A poet since her early teens, she indulges her passions for nature walks, classical music, opera singing, and omnivorous reading. William Blake, Teresa of Avila, Thomas Merton and other of the immortals have been known to break in on her moments of contemplation. She has been married for twenty-three years and has a lively teen-aged daughter. Living in Port Moody, British Columbia, she is currently editing the memoirs of a deceased elderly friend who was her spiritual mentor for nearly twenty years.